A.D.
THE BIBLE CONTINUES

ROMA DOWNEY | MARK BURNETT

TYNDALE HOUSE PUBLISHERS, INC.
CAROL STREAM, ILLINOIS

I T IS OUR PLEASURE to share with you a selection of beautiful photo-graphy from *A.D. The Bible Continues.* We hope these captivating images remind you of your favorite moments in the television event and inspire you to take a scenic journey through the world of *A.D. The Bible Continues.*

The idea for this show began as a discussion on the set of *The Bible* miniseries in 2012. We were having so much fun bringing to life the stories of the Bible that we just didn't want it to end. There was still too much story to tell.

What happened prior to Christ's death is known by millions, but the story of what happened next—how lives were changed following his death and how this revolution that affected world and religious history—is new to many. How did a small group of Jesus-followers spread his Word so successfully that their number has grown to more than two billion strong today?

As storytellers, we know that having the Bible as source material is such a blessing. We turned to the book of Acts to help us frame the series. Acts provided us with a glimpse into how the early church was formed and how a small, steadfast group of followers suffered to spread the Word.

It was an oppressive time for the people in Judea. Controlled by the Roman Empire, the Jews were being suffocated at the hands of foreign occupiers. The Romans were violent and sadistic, crushing all who stood in their way. Yet in this darkest of times, the Word spread through Judea. Those looking for hope were desperate for Jesus' message. It was a time of great change, hope, and miracles.

In the world of *A.D.* The Bible *Continues*, we follow groups who made up the melting pot in first-century Jerusalem. We delve into the world of Caiaphas and the Jewish Temple authorities as they struggled to uphold Jewish law and keep peace with the Romans.

We follow Pontius Pilate and the Roman aristocrats as they tried to understand a world and culture vastly different from their own. We also join Peter and the ever-expanding group of disciples, who preached Jesus' Word in the face of danger. These worlds add culture and texture to an already immersive and exciting story.

The making of *A.D. The Bible Continues* was no easy feat. Starting in May 2014, we began construction on the largest freestanding set in Morocco. It took five hundred local Moroccan construction workers twelve weeks to build the majority of the four major sets: the labyrinthine streets of old-town Jerusalem, the Temple Mount, Pilate's palace, and the thoroughfare of Damascus. It was easy to get lost on set!

Ouarzazate, Morocco, served as our shooting location. A small city surrounded by the majestic Atlas Mountains, Ouarzazate has been the backdrop for many iconic films, such as *Lawrence of Arabia*, *Black Hawk Down*, and *Kingdom of Heaven*. Nicknamed "the doorway to the desert," Ouarzazate was the perfect location for us to recreate life in the first century for *A.D. The Bible Continues*.

Our cast is an incredible mix of actors, all from diverse heritages. In casting *A.D.*, we worked hard to assemble a company of actors who are as multifaceted as Jerusalem was during the first century. The Holy City was the cradle of civilization— a melting pot of culture—and our incredible cast reflects that, as it is composed of more than forty actors from fifteen different countries.

A.D. The Bible Continues is undeniably a tumultuous story of the first followers of Jesus and their dramatic struggle for survival in a complex and dangerous world. Yet amid this violence and intrigue, Jesus' radical message of hope and peace prevailed. It is our hope that this series will change lives all over the world and that people will return to the pages of the Bible to seek his Word.

Through the photography in this book, we invite you to immerse yourself in the world of *A.D. The Bible Continues*. And remember, the Bible is the story that changed the world.

With love and respect,

Roma Downey and Mark Burnett

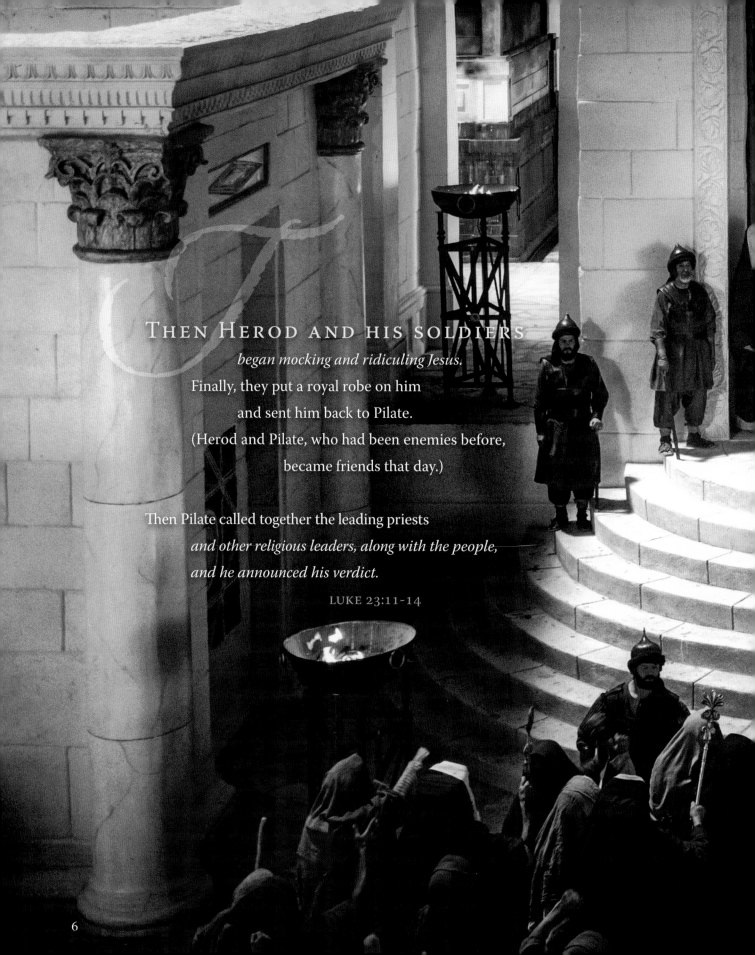

THEN HEROD AND HIS SOLDIERS
began mocking and ridiculing Jesus.
Finally, they put a royal robe on him
and sent him back to Pilate.
(Herod and Pilate, who had been enemies before,
became friends that day.)

Then Pilate called together the leading priests
and other religious leaders, along with the people,
and he announced his verdict.

LUKE 23:11-14

"YOU BROUGHT THIS MAN TO ME,

accusing him of leading a revolt.

I have examined him thoroughly on this point in your presence

and find him innocent.

Herod came to the same conclusion and sent him back to us.

Nothing this man has done calls for the death penalty."

LUKE 23:14-15

PILATE HAD JESUS FLOGGED

with a lead-tipped whip.

THE SOLDIERS WOVE A CROWN OF THORNS

and put it on his head.

JOHN 19:1-2

MANY WOMEN WHO HAD COME FROM GALILEE

with Jesus to care for him

were watching from a distance.

MATTHEW 27:55

VERY EARLY ON SUNDAY MORNING

the women went to the tomb, taking the spices they had prepared.

They found that the stone had been rolled away from the entrance.

So they went in, but they didn't find the body of the Lord Jesus.

As they stood there puzzled, two men suddenly appeared to them,

clothed in dazzling robes.

The women were terrified and bowed with their faces to the ground.

Then the men asked, "Why are you looking among the dead

for someone who is alive? He isn't here! He is risen from the dead!"

LUKE 24:1-6

ONCE WHEN HE WAS EATING WITH THEM,

he commanded them,

"Do not leave Jerusalem until the Father sends you

the gift he promised, as I told you before.

John baptized with water,

but in just a few days you will be baptized with the Holy Spirit."

So when the apostles were with Jesus, they kept asking him,

"Lord, has the time come for you to free Israel

and restore our kingdom?"

He replied, *"The Father alone has the authority*

to set those dates and times, and they are not for you to know.

But you will receive power when the Holy Spirit comes upon you.

And you will be my witnesses, telling people about me everywhere—

in Jerusalem, throughout Judea, in Samaria,

and to the ends of the earth."

ACTS 1:4-8

JESUS APPEARED AGAIN TO THE DISCIPLES

beside the Sea of Galilee.

This is how it happened. Several of the disciples were there—
Simon Peter, Thomas (nicknamed the Twin),
Nathanael from Cana in Galilee, the sons of Zebedee,
and two other disciples.

Simon Peter said, "I'm going fishing."

"We'll come, too," they all said.

So they went out in the boat, but they caught nothing all night.

At dawn Jesus was standing on the beach,

but the disciples couldn't see who he was. He called out,

"Fellows, have you caught any fish?"

"No," they replied.

Then he said, *"Throw out your net on the right-hand side of the boat, and you'll get some!"*

So they did, and they couldn't haul in the net because there were so many fish in it.

Then the disciple Jesus loved said to Peter, "It's the Lord!"

JOHN 21:1-7

All the believers

devoted themselves to the apostles' teaching,

and to fellowship, and to sharing in meals

(including the Lord's Supper), and to prayer.

ACTS 2:42

A DEEP SENSE OF AWE
came over them all,
and the apostles performed many miraculous signs
and wonders.

ACTS 2:43

AND ALL THE BELIEVERS

met together in one place and shared everything they had.

They sold their property and possessions and shared the money with those in need.

They worshiped together at the Temple each day, met in homes for the Lord's Supper,

and shared their meals with great joy and generosity—

all the while praising God and enjoying the goodwill

of all the people.

ACTS 2:44-47

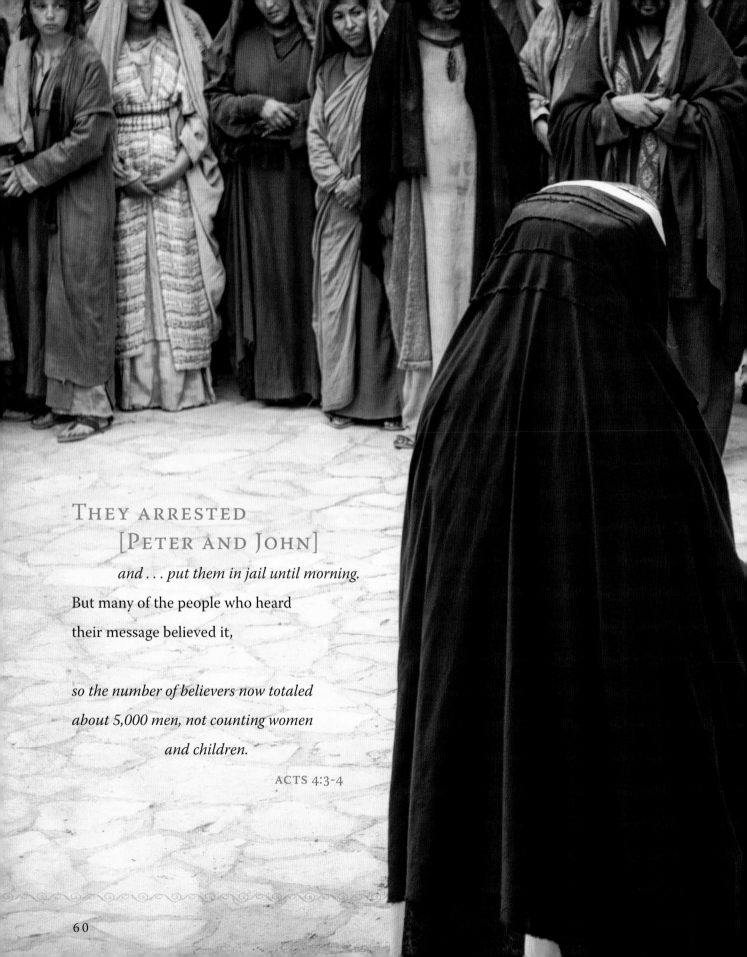

THEY ARRESTED
[PETER AND JOHN]

and . . . put them in jail until morning.

But many of the people who heard

their message believed it,

so the number of believers now totaled

about 5,000 men, not counting women

and children.

ACTS 4:3-4

THE MEMBERS OF THE COUNCIL WERE AMAZED

when they saw the boldness of Peter and John,

for they could see that they were ordinary men

with no special training in the Scriptures.

They also recognized them as men who had been with Jesus.

ACTS 4:13

EACH DAY
the Lord added to their fellowship
those who were being saved.

ACTS 2:27

Peter and John replied,
"DO YOU THINK GOD

wants us to obey you rather than him?
We cannot stop telling about everything
we have seen and heard."

ACTS 4:19-20

As they stoned him, Stephen prayed,
"LORD JESUS, RECEIVE MY SPIRIT."

He fell to his knees, shouting,
"Lord, don't charge them with this sin!"
And with that, he died.

ACTS 7:59-60

SAUL WAS ONE OF THE WITNESSES,
and he agreed completely with the killing of Stephen.
A great wave of persecution began that day,
sweeping over the church in Jerusalem;
and all the believers except the apostles were scattered
through the regions of Judea and Samaria.

ACTS 8:1

Now the people believed

Philip's message of Good News concerning the Kingdom of God
and the name of Jesus Christ.
As a result, many men and women were baptized.

ACTS 8:12

S_{AUL} WAS UTTERING THREATS

with every breath and was eager to kill
the Lord's followers.

So he went to the high priest.

ACTS 9:1

He fell to the ground and heard a voice saying to him,

"SAUL! SAUL!

Why are you persecuting me?"

ACTS 9:4

Something like scales fell from Saul's eyes,

and he regained his sight.

THEN HE GOT UP AND WAS BAPTIZED.

ACTS 9:18

SAUL'S PREACHING

became more and more powerful,

and the Jews in Damascus

couldn't refute his proofs

that Jesus was indeed the Messiah.

ACTS 9:22

THE CHURCH THEN HAD PEACE

throughout Judea, Galilee, and Samaria,

and it became stronger

as the believers lived in the fear of the Lord.

And with the encouragement of the Holy Spirit,

it also grew in numbers.

ACTS 9:31

A.D.
THE BIBLE CONTINUES

Visit Tyndale online at www.tyndale.com.

ShareADTheSeries.com

TYNDALE, Tyndale's quill logo, and *New Living Translation*
are registered trademarks of Tyndale House Publishers, Inc.

A.D. The Bible *Continues*

Published by Tyndale House Publishers, Inc., under license from
Metro-Goldwyn-Mayer Studios, Inc. and LightWorkers Media, LLC.

Photographs used by permission of LightWorkers Media, LLC. All rights reserved.
Design: koechelpeterson.com

Published in association with Dupree/Miller & Associates, Inc.

Scripture quotations are taken from the *Holy Bible*, New Living Translation,
copyright © 1996, 2004, 2007, 2013 by Tyndale House Foundation.
Used by permission of Tyndale House Publishers, Inc., Carol Stream, Illinois 60188.
All rights reserved.

ISBN 978-1-4964-0917-1

Printed in China

15 16 17 18 19 20 21 | | 7 6 5 4 3 2 1